the
WATERHEAD

and other plays

The Waterhead
and other plays

The Big Blue Bird
The Waterhead
Between Mothers

Aaron Bushkowsky

Playwrights Canada Press
Toronto • Canada

Playwrights Canada Press
215 Spadina Avenue, Suite 230, Toronto, Ontario CANADA M5T 2C7
416-703-0013
orders@playwrightscanada.com • www.playwrightscanada.com

Playwrights Canada Press acknowledges the support of
the taxpayers of Canada and the province of Ontario through
The Canada Council for the Arts and the Ontario Arts Council.

Cover painting:"Advent" by Brent Boechler © 2003
Courtesy of Bau-Xi Gallery, Vancouver, British Columbia   www.bau-xi.com
Photo of cover painting taken by Heather Ross.
Production Editor: Jodi Armstrong

National Library of Canada Cataloguing in Publication

Bushkowsky, Aaron, 1957-
    The waterhead and other plays / Aaron Bushkowsky.

Contents: The big blue bird — The Waterhead — Between mothers
ISBN 0-88754-718-4

    I. Title. II. Title: Big blue bird. III. Title: Waterhead.
IV. Title: Between mothers.

PS8553.U69656W37 2004   C812'.54   C2004-900894-3

First edition: February 2004.
Printed and bound by Printco at Toronto, Canada.

to Karen–
who caught up
by reading this

TABLE OF CONTENTS
— — • — — • — —

—•— Playwright's Notes —•—

I like to write about dysfunctional families because I've come from one fairly dysfunctional family. But I don't intend to merely write "what I know." I approach writing from the perspective that I'm writing a piece that I don't know. I try to keep myself open to discoveries and changes with the process that will give the play more dramatic weight, and I look for a moment of transformation where a character is forever changed. This, for me, is the critical moment when the audience, character, and writer all come together. I hope you enjoy these three short plays as much as I enjoyed writing them and watching the actors perform them.

I thank all the people involved in the plays who added their talent, wisdom and perspective to the finished projects. In particular, I thank Tom McBeath, who was involved in each one of these plays as an actor, mentor and director, whose insight was invaluable, and Chapelle Jaffe who helped with her razor-sharp dramaturgy.

For information about past or upcoming shows, please see:
www.solocollective.ca

The Big Blue Bird

The Big Blue Bird won the New Play Centre's 1993 24-hour playwriting competition. It was given a workshop reading in Spring 1994 at the New Play Festival in Vancouver. Robert Clothier played Pieter, Tom McBeath played Herb, and Tim Battle played Len (Lenny). The staged reading was directed by Peter Eliot Weiss.

In 1998 the play received a Equity Co-op production at Vancouver Little Theatre. Don Adams played Herb; Goran Savic played Pieter; and Dirk Van Stralen played Len/Lenny. It was directed by Aaron Bushkowsky. It was nominated for the Jessie Richardson Award for Outstanding Original Play, a Vancouver Professional Theatre Award (Jessies). Set and Lighting Design was by Marti Wright. Set Design was also nominated for a Jessie Theatre Award, while Goran Savic received a nomination for Outstanding Performance.

The Big Blue Bird was a finalist in Theatre BC's National Playwriting Competition, *Theatrum* magazine's centrefold playwriting competition, and the winner of Telefilm Canada's Cross-over Grant of 1994. It was written as a screenplay in 1995.

—•— Characters —•—

Pieter	the Opa, from 50 to 70
Herb	his son, 40s to 60s
Len	Herb's son, in his 20s, then 30s
Lenny	Len as a young child

(LEN and LENNY are played by the same actor. Because this is a memory play the actors may be any age.)

—•— Preface —•—

This play is based somewhat on the plight of my family as they left the German colony they lived on in Russia in 1927. The colony was nearby Kiev in what is now the Ukraine. My grandfather, Opa, had come to Canada to work as a logger to raise enough money to bring his wife and children over from "the old country." But when World War I broke out and the communists in Russia took over, he could not return. He finally returned in 1922, almost seven years after he left. But by that time most of his children were grown up.

My father's siblings refused to accompany the parents to come to what was considered "the promised land" here in Canada. So they left them there. My father and his parents eventually ended up in Winnipeg, Manitoba then moved to Swan River, Manitoba, Canada. They never saw the family they left behind in Russia again.

The story of *The Big Blue Bird* is somewhat different than what actually happened to my family during their move to Canada. It is a story that looks at the missing women in the lives of three men: a grandfather, a father and a son.

It is part memory, part dream. The play takes place, over time, in a small northern town and a larger city, both in Canada. It also takes place back in Russia on a German colony.

The set is fairly bare, but it can suggest a "museum-like" atmosphere with three simple benches.

THE BIG BLUE BIRD

— • — Act One — • —

LEN can enter from off-stage. PIETER and HERB may be lying on benches and could appear either dead or very sound asleep. Or they can enter off stage.

During the play, the two characters act very much like they are part of LEN's imagined past and can remain on stage or in the background.

LEN is 33. It's current time.

LEN
Arden Herodias Linnaeus. The Great Blue Heron. It is usually found on the west coast, ranging from Alaska to BC, to the central states of the USA. It breeds in southeastern Alaska and winters in coastal BC. It is a big blue bird with beautiful plumage that eats little fish and, on rare occasions, a nice butt steak. When Arden Herodias Linnaeus mates, it usually does so for a long time, sometimes for life, and usually without the consent of lawyers, doctors or men of the cloth. It wins the heart of a female by doing a wonderful adaptation of a dance on skates. It's mating call goes exactly like this....

LEN does his best imitation of the mating call. It is lonely and somewhat haunting. He repeats it.

PIETER
(sitting up or entering from the darkness) What the hell was that?

LENNY
(LEN as a seven-year-old) It was my bird call.

PIETER
What kind of bird?

LENNY
I dunno. Almost as big as me and I'm seven, almost eight.

PIETER
Well, what are you waiting for? Go get my gun. We're going to shoot it.

LENNY
I can't get your gun, Opa.

PIETER
> What?

LENNY
> Dad said you shouldn't have "access to any sharp objects or dangerous firearms."

PIETER
> Bastard. Who the hell does he think he is anyway?

LENNY
> Bastard?

PIETER
> It's a big word, don't use it unless you have to. Now come on, let's shake a leg.

> *(PIETER and LENNY are now walking around looking for something.)*

LENNY
> Hey, Dad said we're not supposed to leave the backyard, you know.

PIETER
> Well, I say we can. And I'm older.

LENNY
> Where are we going, anyway?

PIETER
> Backwards.

LENNY
> Oh. *(beat)* What are we looking for?

PIETER
> Our history. And a sharp stick so I can stab that bird over there through her pointy little head.

LENNY
> Why?

PIETER
> Because we gotta eat, don't we?

LENNY
> Well, why don't we just go to Burger King?

PIETER
> Tonight we eat wild meat.

LENNY
Dad says we shouldn't eat wild meat. He said it's ungodly.

PIETER
Look. See? The bedroom light is on again. And your mother's gone for the day. When the cat's away, the mouse will play. That's ungodly.

PIETER pulls out a flask of booze and slugs it back.

LENNY
(beat) Is godly like goodly?

PIETER
Truth is a godly man always, always walks like he's got God in his pants.

LENNY
Gross.

PIETER
See, walk like this.

PIETER walks funny. Perhaps stiffly.

LENNY
I don't think I could do that.

PIETER jams the flask of booze in LENNY's pants.

PIETER
Takes practice Lenny, and it might chafe a bit, but don't give up on it, understand?

LENNY
Hey, I found a stick. A really, really good one.

He shows PIETER.

PIETER
Not bad. Not bad at all. You got a little knife?

LENNY
If I had a little knife why would we need a sharp stick?

PIETER
"Always carry a little knife." Back where I came from you couldn't live without them. See... I grew up on the great steppes of Russia and life was very hard.

LENNY

I've seen those outside the museum. Dad took me. Some of them steps were almost as big as me.

PIETER

(confused) Well, they wasn't as big as the ones around Zhitomar, just outside Kiev in the old country. The old, old country. Miles and miles of nothing but the steppes and wind as big and as mean as.... *(thinks)* When did he take you to that museum, anyway?

LENNY

Last week I think. We drove in to town and shopped and then I watched some guys sticking firecrackers in frogs and then, and then, we went to the park and Dad threw a ball at me and I dropped it and he said if I was gonna do that I should just go on the swing until I got my fill of it and then he told me to get on the merry-go-round and he pushed me around and around and around and around until all the trees were running into each other and the sun was on the wrong side of the sky and then I threw up. *(beat)* It was fun. Really.

PIETER

So, your dad finally played with you?

LENNY

No. He made me throw-up. Aren't you listening? Or did you forget your hearing aid again?

PIETER

I hear fine. In fact, I can hear bees and birds and elk and like I can hear hearts and lungs and blood pumping through veins... I know everything.

LENNY

(pointing at the bird) Hey, look!

PIETER

What?!

LENNY

The bird. It's landing. Look how it walks. Like it's on strings.

> PIETER *prepares to throw the stick at it, but* LENNY *quickly comes to its rescue and* YELLS *at it.*

LENNY

NOOOOOOOO!

HERB

(bolting upright) Hey, what's the racket?

LEN

(from his room) Just the TV.

PIETER fades away.

HERB

Well, turn that thing down. Some of us got to work tomorrow.

LEN

All right. All right.

HERB

(discovers he can't go back to sleep) I can't go back to sleep knowing you're up and lazing about all night with absolutely no idea how you're gonna run your life. I'm not that kind of man.

LEN

I'm learning things about birds. On Letterman.

HERB

Letterman knows nothing about birds. But you put a half-naked woman wearing black nylons in front of him and all of a sudden, he's an expert.

LEN

You should see this. He's got these high-school kids that do bird calls on his show. It's hilarious.

HERB

You're a grown man. Twenty-five years old and you think 12-year-olds doing bird calls on Letterman is hilarious? What kind of child did I raise here? *(Beat. He turns off the TV.)* An unemployed one, living at home on handouts... living off the system...

LEN

Look, we've been over this before, I'm getting my business set up.

HERB

Business? You call that a business? *(no response)* You know, son, there's a few things you should try to remember if you want to be successful in life. One, you can never have too much education. Two, always take a piss before going on any long trips. Three, don't wear brown shoes with black pants. Four, commit your life to God before you fry in hell like my old man.

And five, don't open a greeting card business in a town with less than a hundred people in it. Commit that to memory.

LEN

I'm not gonna give up on my dream. Opa always said...

HERB

Give it up! Please!! It's a dream. Look at me. Do I live on dreams? Not a chance. I have a successful business cleaning pants. And sure, it's not that exciting. It's not that big of a deal. But it's good, honest work. And I learned things. I learned how to make the customer happy. I learned how to deliver the goods on time. I learned how to run a crease straight and true and to the top of a polished shoe. Hey, look at this crease on my pants. Look at it harder. Straight, straight, straight. Even when I walk here to there or anywhere. It's always, always straight. That takes a little practice, you know. You don't just get the line straight overnight. It doesn't just happen by magic. Nothing works like that. You gotta be disciplined. You gotta be exact. You gotta take measurements and write things down. You always gotta write things down. And you gotta work at it one-hundred and ten percent. One-hundred and twenty percent. Two hundred... whatever it takes, day in and day out until you get it absolutely right and the line is exactly that. A line! And you know, inside, you can do it over and over again in your sleep. One line after another, one line after another, pressed to perfection. Now that's a business! Start with a simple job, like cleaning pants or something, and mark my words, the world will march right to your door. Forget big dreams, that's for movie stars.

LEN

Opa always said...

HERB

Don't give me Opa sayings. I've had my fill of them.

LEN

He said...

HERB

I don't wanna hear this!

HERB fades into the background.

LEN

(now older) He said... I think... that the single most important thing is to follow your dream. That's what brought him here. Out of Russia. Into Canada. Following his big dream.

PIETER

(entering) No, no, no. I said, "the single most important thing is to follow the stream." That way you can creep up on the buzzard downwind and heave a pointy stick through her evil bird heart.

LENNY

(as a seven-year-old) Are you awake?

PIETER

If I wasn't awake, would I be talking to you?

LENNY

You fell asleep on the table and knocked your drink over. Then you started yelling with your eyes shut. Dad sometimes does that.

PIETER

When?

LENNY

When he's asleep, silly.

PIETER

And what exactly does he say?

LENNY

He calls for his mommy. Like he's a little kid or something. He goes, you know, "Mommy, Mommy, Mommy!"

PIETER

Your father's a sick man, Lenny. It'd be best to kill him.

LENNY

But I'm only eight.

PIETER

When I was eight, I could kill things with strings and rocks like you wouldn't believe. Once I trapped a wolf. Almost tore my foot off. Had to walk home in the freezing cold, one shoe on, one shoe off, bleeding like a stuck pig. But that's the way things went on the steppes of the motherland.

LENNY

I fell down the steps at church once and almost got killed. Honestly.

Strip music up. LENNY notices that PIETER is looking away watching a stripper.

Hey, what's she doing?

PIETER
> *(watching the bird dance)* A feather dance.

> *Sounds of a bar room up.*

LENNY
> Wow.

PIETER
> She does that to torture the males.

LENNY
> Why?

PIETER
> Because that's what they want.

LENNY
> Why?

PIETER
> Because they're very unhappy and they think there's more to life than there really is and this is one good way to find it.

LENNY
> Why?

PIETER
> Because they've spent their whole lives trying to ruin things for themselves by avoiding things because that's what their fathers did and their fathers' fathers, and their fathers' fathers' fathers and their fathers' fathers' fathers' fathers.

LENNY
> Oh. Okay.

> *He watches the dance.*

> What kind of bird you think she is?

PIETER
> A rare fowl.

LENNY
> Cool...

HERB
> *(suddenly bursting in on them)* HAVE YOU LOST YOUR MIND?! Taking a boy into this place!?

PIETER
> A boy should know a man's heart.

HERB

This is a strip bar! *(music suddenly out)* A STRIP BAR!

PIETER

(noticing the quiet) And I thank you for pointing that out to all the people in here.

HERB

(embarrassed) I'm getting tired of this, Father. Real tired.

PIETER

You should try doing this when you're my age. It's goddamn exhausting.

HERB

(to LENNY) I told you to take a walk with your Opa. I did not tell you to come traipsing in here.

LENNY

But we walked in here. Honest.

HERB

(to PIETER) You are responsible for this!

PIETER

And what exactly are you responsible for? Not your son. That's for damn sure. You never do anything with the boy. A boy needs a father on occasion. It does him good.

HERB

Yeah, like I needed you. *(to LENNY)* Come on, we're leaving.

PIETER

There's a lesson to be learned in here, young man.

HERB

Not from you there isn't!

PIETER

I've taught you many things. I taught you to hunt and fish and throw a ball. I taught you to climb a rope and to take a fall. I taught you to plant a tree and to paddle the sea. I did that and I made it rhyme, too.

HERB

You didn't do anything but keep me from finding out the truth.

PIETER

You don't deserve the truth.

LENNY

I like truth.

HERB

Just wait till we get home. You are in big, big trouble.

LENNY

But I didn't mean to get into trouble...

HERB

"Didn't mean to?" "Didn't mean to?!" The whole neighbourhood knows. THE WHOLE NEIGHBOURHOOD!

LENNY

But Opa ran away. I had to follow him...

HERB

Ran away? You ran away?

PIETER

Truth is, I don't like living with a bastard...

HERB

DON'T YOU CALL ME BASTARD! DON'T YOU DARE! You filthy, disgusting, piece of trash! You are a disgrace to your family and this entire community. A disgrace. Bringing a little boy in here and then gloating about it. I have a mind to... to...

PIETER

To what? Send me away? Lock me up and throw away the key? Yeah, then who's gonna take care of the boy while you're out screwing every married woman from here to the next town? Huh? Who will take care of the little one while you're out sinning? Answer me that, you bastard. Go ahead. Say something. Say something! Oh, what's the use?

> *Both PIETER and HERB fade from the scene. LEN pulls down a giant poster of dinosaur bones during the monologue.*

LEN

That was the first sign. It got worse and worse. I can't sleep lately. So I've been surfing the web a lot late at night. There's been an exciting new trend in the theory of evolution. Some scientists say that birds are the direct descendants of dinosaurs. The Great Blue Heron actually shares many of the same breeding habits of Tyrannosaurus Rex, the fiercest carnivore of them all. But yet as mighty as it was, and as frightening as it was, it too, did a mating dance for the females under the dull bronze of volcanic light, then made love with the wind rolling back its giant hazel eyes.

History. It's a weird science.

It goes way back.

> *PIETER enters tentatively.*

PIETER
Where am I anyway?

LEN
(older again) In a museum.

PIETER
What kind of museum?

LEN
A museum... for people.

PIETER
A people museum? There's hardly anything in here.

LEN
Except for people. People like you and me...

PIETER
People don't belong in museums. They should do something constructive like refinish a table or build a house with a nice garage. In my day we didn't have time for wandering around in big empty buildings unless it was a church. And I didn't even do that. *(beat)* Say, you look awfully, awfully familiar. Should I know you?

LEN
You could say I'm related to you.

PIETER
You don't have my face.

LEN
Look... can I ask you a coupla questions...?

PIETER
(looking at the dinosaur) Not much meat left on those bones. But you put those in some boiling water, add a coupla cabbages and two dozen cloves of garlic and you've got some fine eating ahead of you. *(beat)* That's an old Russian recipe for getting rid of chicken bones.

LEN
Well, this is T-Rex. It'd be a little different...

PIETER
(not cluing in) Looks like a big dumb bird if you ask me.
Somebody probably got him with a big pointy stick.

LEN
Probably, he or she's pre-historic.

PIETER
Well, don't touch it then. You never know what you'll pick up.

LEN
Listen, Opa... I just wanna talk.

PIETER
You sure we haven't met before?

LEN
Sure.

PIETER
How old are you?

LEN
Thirty-something.

PIETER
That's not very old.

LEN
I know. *(beat)* I just want to ask you a coupla things.

PIETER
Why?

LEN
Research.

PIETER
Why?

LEN
So I can sleep better.

PIETER
At your age you should sleep well.

LEN
Yeah, well... I'm just trying to get the story right.

PIETER
From me?

LEN
Sure.

PIETER
What am I all of a sudden? Some kind of expert?

LEN
Yes. I hope you don't mind...

PIETER
Why should I mind? I'm in no hurry. *(beat)* Have you noticed the ceiling in here? Look. It's like a church.

Quickly sings a bit from an old hymn, as if testing out the acoustics.

Very nice. I like the sound in here. It carries very good, up there and all around... very nice. This is a good place to remember a song.

Never mind. Sit. Let's hear your big complicated questions.

LEN
Okay. Why did you come to this country in the first place?

PIETER
Why? Well, let's see. I guess I came to Canada to make some money. Logging forests and trapping all the furry animals I could stomach. Had to make enough money to bring my beautiful wife over from Russia. We had big plans. Such big plans. We were thinking ahead back in those days. Over here, you could still have big dreams.

Let me give you some advice, young man, you find something you're good at and you stick to it, money comes easy if you're doing what you want. And dreams, they come even easier. Look at me. Huh? I've done not too bad, I'd say. This shirt was made in China. The boots... they're made of Ostrich leather. The watch is from guess where...? Poland. *(beat)* What do you do for a living?

LEN
Greeting cards. Mostly for kids. They love dinosaurs, especially on greeting cards.

PIETER
Back in my day, we'd stick our head out the door and yell "HELLO OVER THERE!" Now, that was a greeting.

LEN
Things have changed.

PIETER
So it seems. Now you need cards.

LEN
Tell me more about what you did.

PIETER
Let's see, what did I do back in those days? Well, I chopped down whole forests in the summer, killed as many animals as I could in the winter. Was making nearly six bucks a day, which by the way, was nothing to sneeze at back then. But then war broke out and nobody was allowed to go back and forth. Not for a long, long time.

LEN
What happened to your wife?

PIETER
She worked in the salt mines and in-between learned to dance.

We hear Russian music. A fleeting, soft image of a woman appears behind them.

Danced with her work boots tied around her neck. Danced with her bandaged hands and her blue and red 'kerchief tied around her golden hair...

He grabs LEN and they dance through the light of the projected image of the woman. HERB watches this from the background. PIETER finally releases LEN, who spins away. PIETER then takes HERB and they dance but it turns angry and they struggle with each other. PIETER gives up and spins away. LEN then holds out a hand to dance with his father. But HERB feints at him, laughs and walks away. LEN takes a moment...

LEN
The big problem for me growing up was learning to dance around two fathers. Two times two. Each spoke his own language. Each expected me to interpret for him. Each despised each other. Each to his own. Each and his own. Each, each, each, each, each, each... *(beat)* T'each.

It was a lovely childhood. *(beat)* The women were in the shadows. You could see them move only when you looked away.

When LEN looks back toward the image of the woman, it fades.
LEN gives up and sits down to watch TV. Blue light surrounds him.
HERB watches LEN watch.

HERB
Watching that boob tube again?

LEN
Don't touch that dial.

HERB
Your mind is going to rot.

LEN
Hey, I'm warning you! Don't touch it.

A moment. HERB decides to back off.

HERB
Imagine that. My son telling me what to do in my own house.
That's a sad situation. Very sad.

LEN
Big deal.

HERB
It's a very big deal.

LEN
Look, you mind? I'm watching a documentary. Understand?
A doc-u-men-tary.

HERB
Twenty-seven years old and he talks to his father like he's a child.
You weren't like this when you were younger. You used to watch
that Letterman and get a big laugh. Now it's documentaries.
You've become more cynical. Very sad.

LEN
Please be quiet!

HERB
Very sad indeed.

A long pause. He clears his throat and sings a hymn to himself
quietly. It could be "NEARER MY GOD TO THEE" or something
similar. LEN is irritated. Finally:

LEN
WHY are you singing?

HERB

I was hoping you'd join in.

LEN

Why would I do that?

HERB

I used to sing with your Opa all the time. I'm told I wanted to. Yes sir, we'd sit on the porch in the middle of the night, nothing but a bare lightbulb and the snowflake moths bumping above our cold heads. We'd just sit there and sing every hymn we knew. Yes sir. Those were the days all right. It's nice to do something like that. With your old man.

LEN

I'm getting a little old for that stuff.

HERB

You're never too old. Look at me I'm over 50 and I can sing like a nightingale... *(he sings)*

LEN

Stop it! Please. I don't want to do anything else but what I'm doing right now. So just leave me alone!

HERB

(beat) So you'd rather sit there...

LEN

I'd rather sit here...

HERB

And watch TV...

LEN

And watch TV.

HERB

Period.

LEN

Period!

HERB

(beat) Very, very, sad, sad indeed.

> He watches LEN watch TV. Lights up on PIETER who sings a hymn. HERB tries to join in, gives up. HERB fades and PIETER sings by himself. PIETER fades somewhat. LEN thinks he hears

something, then gives up and lies down on the floor to draw with a felt pen on a giant pad of paper.

LEN

Seven... eight years old. I'm sitting in my room. Playing. By myself. I have something in my hand. A felt pen. Or a crayon. No, it's something else. It's kite string. Fishing line. A piece.... Something wrapped around my fingers. My chest. My head. Around and around and around and around...

He gives up trying to draw. The felt pen silent.

No sound.

HERB

(entering quickly) The phone, the phone! Where is it?!

LENNY

I don't know. Honest.

HERB

This place is a pigsty! An absolute pigsty!

LENNY

I'm not a pig. I'm a boy.

HERB

I've gotta call the RCMP again. They'll have to find him.

LENNY

They won't find him. He's too smart for them.

HERB

He's not that smart.

LENNY

He knows a lot about being outside.

HERB

He knows nothing!

LENNY

He said that if you walk backwards on your footprints, people will get generally confused.

HERB

Where's my gloves...? I'm gonna have to go out there...

Crazy old man. Telling you what's smart and then running away on the coldest day of the year. Where's my coat?

LENNY

He said when he was little he could kill things like you wouldn't believe.

HERB

Killing? He talks about killing things? Idiot.

LENNY

I wouldn't just kill anything. Don't worry I'm not that kind of boy...

HERB

Don't you listen to him. Don't you dare. He's crazy. I have a mind to lock him up and throw away the key.

LENNY

I think Opa hides in the woods because he wants to kill something... or someone.

HERB

What?

LENNY

He hides behind a big rock or a tree and then when you walk by, BANG, he hits you in the head with a big stick and you fall over dead. Opa said forests hide big secrets.

HERB

(*beat*) Well, I'm not going to go out there in the freezing cold to find a crazy man. I won't do that! I'm not that kinda man.

LENNY

He's looking for his Wilamena.

HERB stops suddenly.

HERB

What?!

LENNY

He said he lost her in the snow. Down by the river, or something, I dunno. She worked with salt. Made things outta it and everything and then danced with her shoes tied around her neck. Then everybody clapped.

HERB stops again.

He said she was beautiful. And she made him cry. It's very complicated, you know.

HERB

What does an eight-year-old know about complication?

LENNY

Lots. Really. See, it's complicated cuz Opa came here in the middle of winter to cut down trees and catch animals wearing fur coats and she, Wilamena, that's the mother who lived in the motherland outside these steps in Russia, she was dancing with shoes around her neck waiting for this great big war to be over so they could live happily ever after the end.

HERB

I don't want to hear this... this shit.

LENNY

I write everything down lately. You did notice that, didn't you? I mean, I'm writing things down all the time, just like you...

HERB

OUTSIDE! NOW! OUT! FIND HIM! GO!

LENNY

All right, all right.

> *LENNY leaves and then becomes a much more solemn LEN. He watches his father with a woman in silhouette. Their shadows dance to eerie music.*

LEN

Cold. It's winter. I'm coming home after school. I'm eight. I was in detention or something. It's late. After five. My mother is gone again. Visiting her sick mother in the city. My father's bedroom window light. I can see it four or five blocks away. Shadows. At the window. His shadow twists another shadow that twists back. They move across the movie screen of the window blinds. Every night another woman with the same shadow. They dance. Twisted.

What my father did was habit forming. It was love at its worst.

PIETER

(bolting upright) I tell you what's habit forming. Chewing tobacco! You put it in your lip, then spit a lot. Try it. It's fun!

LENNY

(sticking the chewing tobacco in his mouth) It tastes gross!! Like dog shit.

PIETER

Yeah, but that way you spit more. And there's nothing more satisfying than a good spit. It'll take your mind off the cold. And women.

LENNY

But I'm not cold.

PIETER

Drink more whiskey. Here, have some more. (*gives him rye*) It's fun!

LENNY

I'm not going to get in trouble for this, am I?

PIETER

Naw. It's good for you. Look at me. I'm healthy as a horse.

LENNY

What kind of horse, Opa?

PIETER

One of those horses that pull beer carts around. Got a pecker the size of a spruce.

LENNY

"Pecker?" What's that?

PIETER

Same as penis, except bigger.

LENNY

Oh, pecker! I saw my dad's once and I said what's that? what's that? and he said it's a little bird that's all, just a little bird in my hand. (*beat*) Where are we, anyway?

PIETER

Down by the river. Waiting for old stork legs to come home to roost.

LENNY

Oh. (*beat*) What kind of bird is it? What kind?

PIETER

(*thinks*) Well, it's a Russian name. And it's hard to pronounce.

LENNY

But I'm eight.

PIETER

It was nearly eight years before I saw my lovely wife.

LENNY

I know a bird called the Great Blue Heron. We read about it in school... is that who we're waiting for? Is it?

PIETER

(becoming more solemn) Did I ever tell you where she was taken?

LENNY

Tell me where she was taken. I won't tell anybody, I promise.

PIETER

She was taken away by the Russians. At the point of a gun. A rag stuffed in her mouth. That's what they did to us. Marched us into the interior, away from the steppes, to the back side of the big mountains where the wind blew and blew and blew and blew. And the snow was the colour of stars. And wishes, they'd fall through your hands.

I didn't know what she was doing and she didn't know what I was doing. Here. In another country. How cold it got. How cold and mean that wind got. It drew a map of wrinkles across my face. Sitting on a log in a shack in the middle of nowhere trying to stay warm. I told myself I could wait. I could wait. Inside. Wait. Wait. Wait. And my arms... so heavy. And my chest... so heavy. Like stones. Here and here... and here.

Nobody knew. Not even my Wilamena.

> *PIETER sobs. LENNY doesn't know what to do.*

LENNY

(beat) I'm almost in grade three, you know.

PIETER

Really.

LENNY

Yeah, I'm writing things down all the time.

PIETER

You don't say.

LENNY

You wanna watch me write? *(beat)* You're not listening to me, Opa. I can tell.

PIETER

Have some more chewing tobacco. It'll grow hair on your chest and maybe give you lip cancer. It's fun...

HERB

(*interrupting*) Just what do you think you're doing out here?!!

PIETER

Bird watching.

LENNY

Yeah and spitting tobacco, too. It's fun...

HERB

Spit that out!! Now!

> *LENNY does. HERB to PIETER:*

Imagine taking a little boy down to the river in the middle of winter. For what reason? Well?! WELL?!! (*beat*) That's what I thought, you have nothing to say for yourself, do you? You call yourself a God-fearing man...

PIETER

I've never feared God...

HERB

Teaching a boy to be an alcoholic. Teaching him the worldly ways. What kind of man are you, anyway?

PIETER

I am a grandfather, father, uncle, and now, birdwatcher...

HERB

I know what you are. I KNOW EXACTLY WHAT YOU ARE!

LENNY

Why are you yelling?

HERB

(*cuffing him*) Mind your own business.

> *LENNY backs off sadly.*

PIETER

(*cuffing HERB*) Hey, stop that or I'll really give you something to cry about!

> *LENNY backs away to the shadows and watches as HERB and PIETER become younger. It's a time when HERB was the same age as young LENNY.*

HERB

(*He seems younger.*) Hey, don't hit me... I wasn't doing nothing.

PIETER

You were bothering me. I won't be bothered. Not today. I've got wood to chop.

HERB

But I... I wasn't trying to bother you...

PIETER

What do you want to know? What? What!?

HERB

I just wanna know what happened, that's all.

PIETER

What happened?

HERB

It's my assignment...

PIETER

What for?

HERB

School. We're supposed to write our family history...

PIETER

History? We have no history.

HERB

...for Social Studies. My teacher said I had to...

PIETER

What does a teacher know with his nose stuck in a book all day? He knows nothing. That's what he knows.

HERB

But if you could just tell me...

PIETER

Some things a father can't tell his son. And you better get that through your thick skull! Understand?

HERB

But I'm eight and everybody else in class is doing it... we have to.

PIETER

And if everybody else told you to jump in the lake, would you? WELL? Answer me! This is it, just you and me! Hear me? YOU AND ME!

HERB

    (eventually turning to LEN in the shadows) Did you hear that? Did you? Answer me. Did you hear that? YES OR NO?! Oh, what's the use? What's the use?

    LEN moves to the forefront as HERB and PIETER fade away. LEN is older again.

LEN

    Congratulations. You've chosen a challenging career in Greeting Cards. It's very competitive and you won't get much support, especially from your family. Trust me. But when you strike it rich like Dilbert or Peanuts or Garfield, you'll never look back, well, maybe to see if your yacht is still tied up at the dock.

    The trouble with writing greeting cards is that you have to think about what people might want to say to their so-called loved ones between the lines.

    "We appreciate your firm hand and fine heart,
the way you tried to love us from the start,
As only a father could and should and always will be,
Trying to put love over us like giant, shivering tree."

    I have no idea what the hell that means. Honestly. It was my very first greeting card. Which I gave to my... father.

    He has a little breakdown. He tries to recover.

    I got better though and so will you.

    Anyway... I'm getting carried away here. Where was I? Right...

    Congratulations. You've chosen a challenging career in Greeting Cards. *(beat)* I'm sorry. Uh... sorry. Where was I?

HERB

    (Entering slowly. They are in a seniors' home.) So, what are you up to these days, son?

LEN

    I just dropped in for a minute, you know, to bring you a card...

HERB

    I've always liked your cards.

    He reads the card. He laughs a little.

    That's funny. Real funny. *(beat)* It's supposed to be, right?

LEN
> It can be whatever you want it to be.

HERB
> Well, it's good for a laugh, that's for sure. A little one at least. Right?

LEN
> Right.

HERB
> Right.

LEN
> Right.

> *Beat. An uncomfortable silence. HERB gives the card back because he sees it isn't signed.*

> Well, I just came in to see how you're doing....

HERB
> You don't have much time...?

LEN
> No, I'm going to a convention. Hallmark is sponsoring it.

HERB
> Hallmark? Is that right? *(beat)* Who is he? Should I know the fellow?

LEN
> It's a company, Father.

HERB
> Please, Len... you can call me "Dad." You're not that old. When you get my age, then you can call me "Father." But for now, "Dad" will do. *(beat)* How old are you anyway?

LEN
> Thirty-two.

HERB
> Thirty-two? That can't be.

LEN
> It is. Trust me.

HERB
> Well, you look... twenty-six.

LEN

They treating you okay in here, Father?

HERB

Oh, sure, sure... it's a nice place. 'Cept they always got the thermostat turned down so low and the windows don't open... *(beat)* You know, this is the same place my father stayed in. He was a stubborn one, that one. Wouldn't move in at first. Wanted to stay in our house until he died. Almost did. *(beat)* So how's the wife, Len?

LEN

I'm not married, father. You know that.

HERB

Funny, you look married.

LEN

And how does somebody look when they're married?

HERB

Worried. *(He laughs at his own joke.)* That was a good one. And I thought of it just like that. Still sharp as a duck, right? *(laughs again, beat)* Did I just say "duck?"

LEN

Yes.

HERB

Well, I wonder where that came from?

LEN

We are beside the lake. Maybe you heard one quack or something. Out there.

HERB

Yeah, maybe that's it, all right. Water's ice cold. I guess some of the nurses got out their bathing suits and gave it a try last year. But it's just too cold.

You know, you should try to find yourself a nice woman, settle down. You like women, don't you?

LEN

Of course.

HERB

I don't see you with a lot of women...

LEN
Well, I'm very busy, you know, with the job and everything...

HERB
It's not healthy to be without a woman for very long...

LEN
Yeah, well, I'm very, very busy, that's all...

HERB
It's biblical. To be with a woman.

LEN
I'm sure you believe that.

HERB
It's not a matter of what I believe. It's the truth. *(beat)* How else do you think we're going to populate this great planet of ours? By magic? Families don't grow on trees. It takes commitment, effort and respect. *(beat)* And women. One woman. A mate. Let me give you some advice. You get married, stay married. No hanky-panky. We're not apes. We're more advanced. We're intelligent beings and we know the difference between right and wrong, no matter what other people are saying. Scientists! Psychologists! Those so-called experts! They know absolutely nothing about the human heart. NOTHING!

The way they analyse everything. And when they can't figure out why something isn't going perfect, they blame the family or your upbringing...!

> *He starts coughing.*

LEN
Should I call somebody?

HERB
Oh, just leave them alone. They're crazy in here. All of them. *(beat)* You know what their diagnosis is? They say I have a build-up in my heart. Idiots. All of them. *(beat)* Except for that one pretty nurse who always comes in the morning to give me a sponge bath. She's something, that one. A regular Florence Nightingale. Just beautiful. All that beautiful white, white skin. Sometimes when she leans over to take my blood pressure, her shoulder, up here, touches my cheek. Here. And here. All that white smooth skin on my rough old face. Here. And here...

Now don't you worry about me. I know what the doctor says. "No excitement." Not at my age. Not a chance.

(beat) How old am I, anyway?

LEN
I don't know. Really.

HERB
Well, it doesn't matter. I've lived a good life. Learned a few lessons about the human condition, that's for sure. *(beat)* You want to know the most important lesson I learned? And you won't learn this in any classroom. Come closer. Come on.

> *LEN finds a chair and sits closer.*

Now put your hand on my heart.

> *LEN hesitates.*

Come on! You're not afraid to touch your old man, are you?

> *LEN puts his hand on his father's heart.*

The most important lesson of the human condition is to be trustworthy. You understand me? Trustworthy! To be worthy of trust like you wouldn't believe. To be left to your own vices and to be flawless, to be honourable, to be above reproach. To be a really nice guy.

> *Beat.*

That's the straight goods.

> *Beat.*

You understand what I'm saying?

LEN
Yes.

HERB
No. I want you to say it.

LEN
Look, Dad...

HERB
Say it aloud! Come on. For me.

LEN
(hesitantly) The most important lesson...

HERB
Of the human condition...

LEN

Of the human condition is to be trustworthy.

HERB

Very good. Now get your hand outta there. Your fingers are like icicles. I can hardly breathe.

You should write that lesson down somewhere, use it in your writing.

LEN

I will.

LEN gets ready to leave.

HERB

I've read your writing. In the cards. Like this one. I don't always understand them, but they sure are different. You know, I tell the nurses here you were born with stars in your eyes and a pen in your mouth. That always gets a big laugh.

LEN

Thank you very much.

HERB

You write things like nobody's business. And that's a good thing. People wanna read stories, people wanna know histories.

That's the magic of words. One line to another. And so it goes. I just wish your mother could be.... She was always so well-read. Always had a book full of pressed flowers under her arm. Always knew this thing and that and whatever you could think of. Even knew what I was up to from just holding my hand. Imagine that. Just from holding my hand. She knew...

A moment.

Good God it's cold in here. Like I'm lying outside in the snow or something.

HERB looks sick and weak and pathetic.

LEN

Why didn't you two work things out? What happened?

HERB

What happened, happened. She hadda do what she hadda do. It's a sad story. Sad and full of trash. I wish it was otherwise, son. Anyway, I think you probably know.

LEN
(*beat*) What was she like? Tell me again.

LEN sits to hear the story.

HERB
Oh, she was some catch all right. A nice woman to boot, met her at church... she was in the choir. She was wearing this dress the colour of.... Well, it just caught my eye. She was a very appreciable woman.

Always knew the name of a song even if you hummed a coupla bars or tapped out the beat with the ring on your wedding finger. I think that's where you got your artistic side from.

Oh, you would have liked her, all right. I'm sorry she left like she did. But that was partly my fault, I'd say. Partly mine and partly hers the way we parted.

I was a bit of a bad apple in those days. And sometimes I wish it wasn't so. But it is. Sad to say and full of trash, all right.

Beat. Looks tired and lies down.

Why I am always so tired, these days? It seems that all I do is eat, sleep and dream. Eat, sleep, dream... eat, sleep, dream...

He sleeps.

LEN
So, what do you dream about... Dad? Dad?

(*beat*) Are you there? Dad?

There is no answer. LEN signs the card and puts it on top of HERB's chest and moves away slowly.

LEN moves to centre-stage as HERB leaves.

The other day I read this article in one of his magazines. *National Geographic.* They followed him to the very end....
I found crates and crates of them. In his closet, under the bed, in the basement, upstairs, everywhere. My stuff now, I guess.

Anyway, it said that in the early sixties scientists discovered to their dismay that the whooping crane was nearly extinct. A concerted effort was made to save the species. Eggs were taken from their nests and secretly put into the nests of the much more common sand crane. This particular species had less than half the migratory distance to cover and supposedly were much better parents. As a result, the whooping crane made a little bit of a come-back.

But, not only were scientists shocked to find out that they had inadvertently created a new bastard type of bird, which was an unfortunate mix of sand and whooping crane, it was even more of a shock when they discovered that the numbers of the whooping crane, even hundreds of years ago, were still about the same. Between one or two hundred. Believe it or not, as a species these big birds had learned to survive with the smallest of numbers.

HERB
(entering) What are you doing down there in the dark?

LEN
Surviving.

HERB
It's like a tomb. You can't survive in a tomb, it's bad for you.

LEN
Go away.

HERB
You'll pick something up...

LEN
I'm trying to sleep! Please!

A moment.

HERB
You mad at me?

LEN
Why would I be mad at you?

HERB
I dunno. Just seems the older you get, the more you're mad at me. I'm just wondering if this happens to all parents.

How old are you now anyway? Thirty-one? Isn't your birthday coming up?

No answer.

You're weren't this way when you were young. Everybody said you looked like the happiest kid around....

LEN
Look. I've had a bad day.

HERB
You've had a bad day?

LEN
Yeah.

HERB
What kind of bad day?

LEN
A very bad day.

HERB
What kind of very bad day?

LEN
A very, very bad, bad day.

HERB
What kind–?

LEN
(trying) A shipment was late, I had to fire an employee, then the water pipe broke and ruined $3,000 worth of merchandise, then I got cited by the fire department for blocking an entrance or something. And to top it off, somebody vandalized the storeroom. They sprayed "Bad Karma" on the wall in red paint. They spelled it with a "C."

HERB
Well, that's life. I remember when my father got hit by an axe – now that's a bad day!

LEN
Listen, just leave and close the door. I want to nap.

HERB
Naps are for cats.

LEN
(to himself) Oh, God... God... God...

HERB
Look at the time, look at the time. (beat) Do you even know what day it is?!

LEN
Please, could you just...

HERB
Twenty years to the day that your mother left. For good.

No answer.

She said someday I should take the time and explain her.... My actions. Plus I haven't been feeling so well myself.

LEN
Look, father–

HERB
Oh, I get the occasional sharp pain shooting up my arm. A long, winding knife to my heart. Ah, nothing I can't handle. But you never know how much time you have. When the Good Lord calls you'd better get your house in order, I always say.

No answer.

There's a ball game on TV. The Blue Jays are playing. *(beat)* You always liked ball games, right?

No answer.

Remember that time we went to the park? I think you were seven... maybe eight. *(beat)* You remember if we played on the merry-go-round?

No answer. HERB picks up a phone.

HERB
Here. Phone your girlfriend. You're depressed.

LEN
I thought you were going to explain my mother. Explain away.

HERB
(jamming the phone into LEN's hands) Phone a girlfriend first!

LEN
I don't have a girlfriend.

HERB
Well, get one. There must be thousands out there.

LEN
I'm not phoning anybody.

HERB
PHONE A GIRL! DO IT!

LEN

(putting the phone down empathetically) I'm leaving.

> *HERB grabs him but LEN throws his arms off.*

You're too old for that and so am I.

> *LEN goes to leave, but turns around and stares HERB down until he leaves. PIETER walks out drinking and sits. LEN becomes LENNY and walks around "outside" until he finds PIETER drinking.*

PIETER

What are you doing here?

LENNY

I'm going to run away with you. I like you.

PIETER

That's beautiful. *(They embrace.)* You're the boy I never had. And you're as innocent as the day is long. That's why I'm here. I will change all that.

LENNY

Why?

PIETER

Because people will hurt you. You gotta learn that.

LENNY

Why?

PIETER

Because hurting is part of our nature.

LENNY

Look what happened to me today. *(shows him a bruise)*

PIETER

He hasn't learned anything. He's just got the disease of unhappiness and it's eating him alive.

> *PIETER takes off his shirt and pants.*

LENNY

Hey, you're taking off your clothes. How come?

PIETER

I'm gonna jump in the water and catch me a big blue water bird. You should try it, it's fun!

LENNY
> *(stripping down to his underwear too)* Isn't it kinda cold for that?

PIETER
> It's only winter. The best time to catch these big dumb birds napping.

LENNY
> I'm not gonna get in trouble for this, am I?

PIETER
> You wanna catch a bird in the act, don't you?

LENNY
> Yeah. *(thinks)* What act?

PIETER
> *(sizing up the bird)* The worst act possible.

LENNY
> Wow. *(sizing up the bird)*

PIETER
> Hurry up! Come on. We don't have all day.

> *They stalk the bird. It dances a bit. HERB gets up, sees what's happening and stalks PIETER and LENNY who are, in turn, stalking the bird.*

> See, I've done this before. And the trick is to sneak up on her with a song on your heart. You got a song on your heart?

LENNY
> Yeah, I guess.

PIETER
> Good. Come with me across the steppes of the great motherland. The place with a million lakes. Where owls twist their heads and eagles stay awake.

LENNY
> Me too.

PIETER
> And I got a song on my heart and pocket full of cash. I'm gonna rescue my loved one from the wrong side of the mountains. I'm gonna take her to her new home where people talk funny.

LENNY
> Me too.

PIETER

I'm gonna take her by the hand and hold her in my arms, dance all the way back to Winnipeg, Manitoba. The Promised Land!

LENNY

Yeah!

PIETER swings LENNY around.

PIETER

And it's been eight long years and I'm just dying to meet her.

LENNY

Me too!

PIETER

And I round the corner and what do I find?

LENNY

I don't know. What?

PIETER

And I round the corner and what do I find?

LENNY

I dunno. What!? What?!

PIETER

I find a son that's no son of mine.

PIETER faces HERB at seven.

HERB

Who are you?

PIETER

Who are you?!

HERB

Herb. I'm seven.

PIETER

No. You're a bastard! A goddamned bastard! *(to LENNY)* Come on, we're leaving without the bird.

LENNY

Why?

PIETER

Because some birds can hurt you.

HERB

Why are you taking me? I didn't do anything...

PIETER

(to LENNY) Here put your clothes on before you catch your death of colds.

LENNY

I'm getting used to it. Really.

PIETER

(getting clothes on) Just get dressed. We're leaving!!

HERB

I want her to come along! I don't want to go without her.

PIETER

(to LENNY) Get moving! We're leaving!

HERB

But I want her too! She's with me! I'm with her! I am! Really I am!

PIETER

(to LENNY) Just ignore him. He's just a cry-baby.

HERB

I am not a cry-baby! I just want her to come along. That's all. *(beat)* Me, you and her. We could be a family. We could be. Honest.

PIETER

Ha! That's what you think.

LENNY

I think you should let the mother come along.

PIETER

She stays here!! With her cheap perfume and her cabbage and chicken bone soup and her goddamn paying customers. She can dance her whore-dance til the cows come home. It won't matter to me. I don't need no whore. No sir! Not in a million years!

LENNY

But he's just a kid, like me.

PIETER

I don't care. She can't have her bastard. NEVER!! Understand!? Never! I was trapped over there for eight years. Trapped! And when I finally made it back to the old country she wasn't the same Wilamena. She wasn't. And you weren't my child. SHE DIDN'T WAIT! And I did everything I could. Sitting under all that snow, boiling water, using the same tea bags over and over again. Counting days and hours and minutes. All that waiting made me old.

I will not forget everything. I will not walk away. I will have my say. I will make my stand and the world will see the man inside of me. THE MAN INSIDE! And nobody can take that away from me. Nobody, not even God Himself.

(Beat. PIETER is empty.) I have to lie down now. I'm cold. Cold, cold, cold to the very bone.

He lies down.

Is it snowing in here?

HERB
You can't do this to me. You can't. I'm not through with you yet.

PIETER
Leave an old man alone to his thoughts.

HERB
You can't do this to me!

PIETER
Don't come so close.

HERB
We're a family! Families stick together, no matter what. They always, always stick together. And we are no different.

PIETER
Leave me alone!

HERB
My whole life, a mess because you wanted to get even with a woman who couldn't wait eight years. Eight years! That's a lifetime. You can't hold somebody to a lifetime. Not even the strongest vow could hold through that. You might as well ask for the sun and moon. Or the stars for that matter. You can't ask for the impossible. You can't do that.

PIETER
Please. I can't breathe when you're this close.

HERB
She did the best she could.

PIETER
Listen to me...

HERB
She was just trying to survive.

PIETER
Please...

HERB
She did what she had to do! That's all.

PIETER
Listen son... before I go... I want you to promise to quit your bad habits. Find a nice woman, marry her and stick to her... don't go wandering off in the middle of the night. Promise me...

HERB
Please, father... I don't need to hear this...

PIETER
Don't leave her wondering. Don't leave her holding her breath. Don't leave her watching and waiting for the rising of the sun. Don't...

I'm so cold. Why is that? Did you turn down the thermostat again?

LEN
I've told them to turn it up.

PIETER
Well, tell them again. They're stupid in here. Health care workers... they call themselves.... You tell them... they'll listen to you... you're young... YOU TELL THEM–

PIETER coughs.

LEN
Save your strength, Opa.

PIETER
Why?

HERB
Because we need you around.

PIETER
Why?

HERB
Because I was with you, you were with me.

PIETER
(*weaker*) Why?

HERB
Cuz I grew up with you!

PIETER
Why?

HERB
Cuz that's the way things were back then and I got used to that and I'm not ready for you to go yet.

PIETER
Why?

HERB
Cuz I... I appreciate you. I know you, you know me.

PIETER
Why?

HERB
Why? Why? Why? Because we are family. Family. Father, son. Son, father. You and me and me and you! The two of us! We are here. Don't you get it? Don't you understand? (*beat*) Don't you understand.

> *He leaves and sits down on the opposite bench. He watches LEN support PIETER's head to comfort him.*

Leave him alone. That's what he wants, anyway. To be alone. And maybe that's what he deserves, too.

LEN
Don't be so hard on him.

HERB
Don't fool yourself. He is as evil as evil can get. And he's turning you, turning you against me. You're over thirty and he's fooling you with his crazy talk.

LEN
He's not.

HERB
I tell you he is! And you better watch it cuz you're gonna end up like that. Just like that. Stubborn and stupid and selfish and a poor excuse. A poor excuse. For a father.

LEN
(beat) We can go birdwatching, Opa.

HERB
You won't go anywhere with him. Not anymore.

HERB lies down on the opposite bench. He's spent too.

LEN
Opa, please. Just like we did before. Remember? The big, blue bird in the middle of winter...

There is no response.

We can go down, down the river, behind all the beautiful hoar frost trees, under the pinlight stars in the winter breeze that paints us cold. Hold our breath, Opa. Hold our breath. Shake our knees. And wait. Wait.

PIETER
(barely audible) Why?

LEN
Because they sing. They sing even at night.

PIETER
(whispers in LEN's ear) Sing...

PIETER falls back dead.

LEN feels his heart, then for air coming out of his mouth or nose, and finally he closes PIETER's eyes. He leans over slowly and kisses PIETER on the forehead. Then LEN slowly raises his head and gives a long, horrible cry of anguish. It's close to the same bird sound he made at the beginning of the play, but it's definitely more human. HERB looks up and over at LEN. Then he closes his eyes and appears to be dead too. LEN tries to repeat the cry but little comes out.... LEN feels the weight of the world on him. He looks around for hope and gets it when he hears the faint call of a bird joined by the calls of more and more birds until the place is filled with their calls. Behind LEN on the wall or screen we see the image of a giant blue bird. It seems to float in the air in mid-take-off. Lights slowly fade as we go to black.

The end.

The Waterhead

The Waterhead was presented in October 2000 by Solo Collective Theatre at Playwrights Theatre Centre in Vancouver as Part of Solo Collective's *Three By Three* and the *See Seven* independent theatre program. It was performed by Tom McBeath, directed by Del Surjik. Lighting and Set Design by Del Surjik. Stage manager was Karin Fehr.

The Waterhead was nominated for several Jessie Richardson Awards, they included Outstanding Actor, Outstanding Director and Outstanding Production. It won the Jessie Richardson Theatre Award for Outstanding Original Play.

Originally written as a short story, this piece was broadcast, in part, on CBC Radio.

THE WATERHEAD

Lights up, revealing a MAN. A glass of water with an accompanying pitcher of water sit on a nearby red table, which is set for four. The MAN looks around the room.

MAN

What a lot of sad, sad faces. Pathetic really. Haven't got anything better to do? Ridiculous.

I am nine years old and this is the first thing I hear Sunday morning from my father. He's over there making a breakfast of little sausages, pancakes and runny eggs while we slip into our assigned places around the table, ghost-like, our heads still lingering with dreams. Except for me. The smell of grease hurts my eyes and my head aches. The table trumpets its red colour. I'm dying for a coffee but I'm only nine years old. When I'm 39 I'll quit drinking coffee and take up expensive wine.

For now though, I'm nine. I sit down, and hold my head in my hand, the cool of the table on the edge of my funny bone. It's at this moment I realize how quiet my sisters are. Watching my father stir the batter to death, they play with the ringlets in their hair. He shuffles from one side of the stove to the other, from one leg to another, his slippers stroking the floor. Shh-shh. Shh-shh.

A fly lands in the sugar bowl and then, as if knowing what would happen next, flies off.

My father turns around and faces us, wooden spoon dripping batter down his hand, down his brown corduroy pants, onto the floor. He clears his throat, wipes at his eyes with a flour-tipped forefinger that leaves a small "X" near his nose, and says, "Last night your mother came home from the hospital. Your baby sister was born a waterhead. She went quietly right after we named her."

Named her? Named her what? And a waterhead? Why water instead of a brain... or a thought... or an idea? Or anything? This is too weird. I mean, we have brains, don't we?

Not this one, he says.

Oh.

My father goes back to the stove and pours the first pancake. My sisters, sad and considerate from a very early age, ask gently, the name, what's the name? But nothing... my father is busy now. He's taking care of us. "Smile... who wants pancakes?"

When I see my sisters now, sagging and on the edge of being grandmothers, they talk about the pancakes, and how good they tasted that morning, July 23, 1967. Then they stare out the window, a different window, same sky, and sink into big, long, boring conversations while their children sit under the trees, smoking, spitting at the leaves and comparing scars.

To get away from them I take up paddling. I own a sea kayak and I go out onto the water as often as I can. I'm out there right now, fighting the current, digging my paddle in one side then the other, my back leaning into it, my arms and shoulders screaming in pain. I will make it. I will beat my last time, I will win at all costs because I am solid. I am a man and I am solid. I come from solid stock. My father was also a man. He was solid too. An iceberg drifting along some forgotten coast, the unsaid lurking below the surface. Solid. More than me, that's for sure. Oh I have my moments. I see long distance runners finishing a race and they're wobbling, falling down, getting up, fighting to finish and their lovers are screaming at them from behind the finish line, "Come on, you can do it... I love you... come on." And they fall into their arms. It's over. They've done it. Finished. And even the announcers are bawling. Not me, though. I'm solid. Sort of.

My mother, now... well, my mother was constantly sad. She cried oceans. Sometimes I thought the oceans would creep up and drown us at night. My father said we just had to weather the storm and we did. At night I welded my eyes shut and watched the back of my eyelids turn into deserts. I sang songs, counted sheep, slowed my heart and promised myself I would never be like my parents. One solid, one liquid. I thought I was flexible, capable of changing my density.

I was wrong.

My parents live in a basement suite where the humidifier and the thermostat work in combination to recreate Ecuador. Mom and Dad wear sweaters and drink cranberry juice and take massive quantities of pills. For fun they take off their sweaters and throw slippers at each other. They've been doing this for 50 years.

Recently my mother's kidneys gave out. The doctors said she had one too many babies. The last one, the dead one, stole time from her over-worked organs.

I find myself in a hospital. A long white corridor.

People in the halls look like they have just stumbled out of coffins, shuffling along the handrails, heads down, their skin as thin as rice-paper, a welcoming party of the dying and nearly dead. I feel like taking everybody out for a Big Mac. Get some colour in their cheeks. One of them touches my sleeve: "Help me, please, please help me..."

I compose myself near a nursing station, drinking loudly from a shiny water fountain. The hospital blares at me with its whiteness, its sick pine-tree smell tainted with more than a touch of urine, its updated Musak, Bob James doing a Beatles medley—yeah-yeah-yeah—its web of hallways and rooms, sickness and death and dying hiding behind grey curtains, and nobody seems to mind. What's wrong with these people?

When we get to her room, my mother's appearance snaps me out of it. Tubes! Tubes linking her to a bank of blinking machines, liquids steadily dripping from two bags hanging like old woman's teats above her head, her urine—liquid gold, she says—being siphoned off to another bag beside her bed.

She sees me and my lovely wife beside me and smiles. The transplant is working. The new kidney—a donation from a motorcyclist, a dead motorcyclist, she speculates—is slowly drawing the ocean from inside her to the see-through containers that surround her bed. She is making tributaries, tiny bays of herself, run-offs of DNA, blood, puke and sweat and who-knows-what and she knows I can't stand to see her like this, calmly draining her insides for everybody to see and I want to tell my wife I can't take it anymore, I want to tell her I'm scared and embarrassed and sick of thinking we're all going to die some day and I just want to go home and eat popcorn, watch "Baywatch" and forget about everything. Just forget I was ever born because some day, I know this will be me on a different machine. Same kidneys I'm afraid.

Then my mother sees me frowning and fidgeting and looking around at the get-well cards, the semi-dry flowers guarding the window near the fire extinguisher, the tiny dead TV hanging like a snake from the ceiling, and she licks her dry lips and points at me with a shaking, grey finger.

"I'm going to live," she says weakly. "It's a nice feeling. I just hope this doesn't happen to you."

And then she falls asleep.

April showers. You smell them first. At the door. An ambulance is unloading a shrouded body. Lots and lots of silence... for a hospital entrance. So we leave, the hospital smell lingering in our coats as we trudge home through the rain, thinking one of us has to say something, one of us must say something. But I'm in total control, counting my steps, careful not to step on any cracks.

My wife says she does all the crying for both of us and she doesn't actually want the job anymore.

While my mother recovers in the hospital, my father disappears for days at a time. Fishing at the trailer, he tells us long distance over the phone from Spirit Lake, while we worry out loud about my mother feeling alone.

"She's not in very good shape to see me," he explains, over a frying pan of sizzling fish. "I'll let her recover, get her senses, before throwing myself on her."

"Dad" I say...

(as DAD:) "I'll let her recover...

"Dad" I say...

(as DAD:) "What's wrong, are you deaf?"

He's late for pickerel, he has to go. Click.

I have this image of my father. His back is toward me. He's walking along the shore, rod and reel in one hand, in the other, a large pickerel. He's holding it like this. A thumb and finger jammed into the eye sockets of the fish. The tail makes an upside down question mark.

You see, you can't hold a pickerel anywhere else. Its dorsel fin could cut through your hand like butter. But then I've never actually held a fish. They're too much like snakes and lizards combined. Except stupider. And that's probably why we eat them. That's the price you pay for being really dumb and delicious.

So my father stays at the lake. I keep my mother company, help her count her get-well cards, marvel with her at the bag of piss beside her bed, and brush her hair. Beside her an elderly man, shrunken and ghastly-white, struggles to breathe. A respirator strapped over his mouth mists over every ten seconds or so. Occasionally, he claws at the mouthpiece with his one free hand

and barks... a dying animal in the snowy woods, across the thicket, behind the barn. It fades. There are no cards or flowers around his bed. He is forgotten, or maybe he is the one who is left and remembers. I try to block him out, erase the dying sound, fill the space so my mother will relax at least.

"What's it like being in here."

"What do you think?" my mother says.

The old man coughs.

"How's Dad taking it?"

"It's not easy being married to someone like your father," she says. "He's got his schedule and he doesn't like surprises. I guess the operation threw him a curve."

The old man coughs again. I start to sweat.

"God this place smells of piss," I say.

"Yeah," she says, "isn't it great?"

My mother watches me watch out of the window, pigeons at the hospital entrance fighting over breadcrumbs being tossed to them by a small child bundled up in a wheelchair, swaths of green scarfs circling his head, one end flapping in the stiff breeze. I decide that the child is terminally ill, and the parent, dutifully standing behind the wheelchair, realizes that sitting outside in the cold wind doesn't really matter anymore.

"I think I'll go out to the lake," I say quickly. "I'm worried, that's all."

"Well, children shouldn't check up on their parents," my mother snorts. "It doesn't work that way."

A nurse drifts into the room, shark-like. She pulls the curtain around the patient beside my mother and I soon hear what I imagine to be slapping sounds.

Smack.

"When I first met your father he was very secretive. He told me it ran in the family. His father was in the war. Intelligence."

Smack!

"Just before you were born, your father went to Regina a lot. He had a very ill cousin. At least that's what he said."

Smack!

"The insurance business makes schedules part of your life. He often got calls in the middle of the night, in the middle of winter, and he never complained. Never!"

Smack!

I leave. Outside my cheeks are stinging.

I get home and find my wife describing her vomit in the washroom.

I tell her to stop. She says I don't understand.

I don't. I'm going to be a father. I can't breathe. What if the kid is... well, your mind races even at my age. Particularly at my age.

Bloated from the ankles up, my wife suspects she is a twin factory and will ask the doctor to check. And then she says it. Ultrasound. Oh God... I don't want to see this child. I don't want to know anything about it. No way.

At seven in the morning, my wife comes downstairs and says. "Be ultra careful this morning. It's going to be ultra slippery out there."

On the highway to Spirit Lake it starts to rain. The ultra new wiper blades quickly and cleanly throw the ultra rainwater off the ultra windshield and, and–

Shit. This is the way I cope. I don't know where I picked this up – certainly not from my parents. And definitely not my wife who only fills her mind with big angry things and then never tells me about them until it's ULTRA TOO LATE!

I don't want to be a father. I can't be a father. I don't know the first thing about the job. What if this child ends up like me? Or my sisters... what if, what if... the child could die, or hate me.

God, I'm thirsty. I'm always thirsty.

My doctor says I should drink eight glasses of water a day. Hydrate yourself. Liquify. Feel good about everything. Especially when your pee is clear.

God, why is it raining so much these days?

I need music. I really need some music. I open the glove compartment to get a tape. And then it happens. The photo... the photo... tumbles onto the floor mat. I keep my eyes on the road, in front of me a tractor trailer sends a storm of water behind huge tires. I can't see and I don't want to take chances.

The photo though.... Sits. And. Waits. The Waterhead. Dead and lying at my feet.

The thing is about the polaroid. Well, okay, my sisters and I are sitting around the breakfast table July 23, 1967 watching my father weep and nobody wants to say anything because if anybody talks we will all cry and then there will be no control and we can't have that.

We're German.

So we sit, patiently waiting for his tears to stop so one of us can have our turn. He reaches into his breast pocket to get what we think is a hanky or a tissue but it turns out to be a polaroid and he snaps it on the table like a black ace and at first we're not sure what it means. The colours are weird. It's unfocused. A window in the background has caught the flash.

We huddle over the shot, turning it in our hands, studying the pink child, also dressed in pink, lying in the open incubator. A sad nurse with very red eyes stares down at the child. She has her hand over her mouth. The baby has no expression. It is not crying, or in pain, or happy, or anything. It is a blank baby. An angel in waiting. A sliver of light in its eyes, tightly flanked on either side by tiny, tiny clenched fists. Its hair, thin and brown like mine. There is a thin smear of blood on its forehead, like a Hindu mark. Bindi. It's called Bindi. How did I remember that?

Beside the baby, on the blanket covered by little pink unicorns, is a miniature teddy bear that sits in a miniature canoe, paddle ready in its paws.

Summers came and went and we all got tired of wondering and arguing and thinking "what if? what if?"

I ended up with the photo. And the questions.

The truck turns off.

I reach over and pick up the photo. How the hell did that get there? I throw it back into the glove compartment.

As the rain subsides, I drive down a long, sloping hill, turn east toward the darker part of the sky, and follow the dirt road toward the trailers perched at the water's edge, past the abandoned grocery, the empty cabins, the closed gas station, rainwater billowing out behind my Honda like a black parachute.

I coast up to the trailer quietly, turning off the engine before the tires stop rolling. I notice two cars sitting in front of the now rusty Airstream: my father's trusty blue Ford, and a silver Jetta. Shit, he's out fishing with a buddy. No, the boat's at the dock. I get out and stretch, keeping my eyes on the glowing windows at the front of the trailer. Nothing. I jingle some change.

I wish he was out fishing. I could wave at him from shore on his way in, break the ice from a distance. Why am I here? What do I want him to do? Hell, I don't know.

I run a hand through my hair, then walk toward the Airstream. I stop, lean against the door for a moment, waiting to hear something, anything from inside. I should go. A canoe scrapes into the shore down on the beach. Crickets start a choir. Someone yells a mile away across the lake.

A deep breath.

I turn the knob and pull the door open. Inside on the bed in the back, my father naked and white lies on top of another equally white and naked woman. His ass, blotched red and white, jackknives into the air. I'm surprised at how small and hairless it is, ultra small, ultra smooth, like the head of a baby seal. Yes my father, my aged father is humping another woman, also aged.

I say, "Oh my gawd." Twice. My lunch moves up my throat. "Shit."

They stop, look up, mouths open. They see that I see them, but they don't move, two wolves watching from the distance. They're panting.

I stumble back to my car, get in, and start the motor before my father has a chance to get to the door. I see him in the rearview mirror, stumbling from the trailer, his hands over his... cock. I spin my tires. I see my dirt settling around him like dirt should. He lifts his arms and I think he's screaming. But I don't give a shit. Because from now on, he's the old man... not my father.

When I hit the highway, it starts to pour. Lightning flashes knocking songs off the radio and I can't breathe, my head pounding.

Shit. This is it, I think. This is how it all goes. My father, in his late sixties, finally finding relief, my mother, tied to machines, finding life, and me, somewhere between the city and Spirit Lake, with a thundering headache dying for a drink. Christ... I didn't ask for this. I didn't want this. You can't do this to me. I am solid, alright. I am SOLID!

I'm trying to hit the open water before heading back to visit my mother in the hospital. She's improving. Her piss pouring out of her now like a Grecian fountain. She tells me she's writing a sonnet about it.

I'm in the kayak following the water around West Van. I'm waist deep in the stuff, protected by a very thin hull. Rich people wave at me from their verandas. I think one of them is Bryan Adams. He lives there between songs. So does Chong of Cheech and Chong fame. He's the one smoking a big fattie over there.

I hit wave after wave, feeling the cold wash over me, so that my heart starts pounding at the door of my chest. BANG-BANG!

A child in a yellow slicker races along the shore, waving madly at me to either come in or go out.

(as CHILD:) "Hey, you...! Hey, you...!"

A wave crests in front of me.

It passes under the kayak and I sink into the heart of the ocean and it's dark and scary.

I disappear. Another swell. Look back at the shore.... And the child is gone.

(as himself:) "You got to do this.... You got to do this...."

I'm loading the kayak onto the car. Tying it off with my nearly frozen fingers.

"You've got to do this.... You need to do this. You have to."

And I do.

The hospital. I park. I go in and take the stairs.

When I reach the fourth floor, the ICU, I'm out of air, OUT OF AIR! I'm not breathing. I burst from the hall door gasping and gulping, running smack into a nurse. "You okay?" she asks me. I hesitate, embarrassed, nod yes and back away toward my mother, careful not to step on any cracks.

I go to the room, my stomach growling softly under the green sweater I got from my wife four Christmases ago.

I walk in to see my mother in her hospital gown sitting up in bed, her back exposed to me. I've never seen my mother's naked back just like I'd never seen my father's naked butt and I'm not sure what to make of it, moles, a thin scar running across here and tiny white hairs and.... She hears me shuffle my feet and slowly, very slowly turns around, one hand braced against the IV pole.

"I was worried about you," she says calmly, "Where were you?"

"Up at the lake."

My mother carefully positions herself back on the bed. She then stretches out her hands toward me, as if trying to hold the air. "I should have warned you," she said. "He doesn't like to be surprised out at the trailer. It's his special place by the water."

I look down, she looks up, studying the ceiling panelling.

"It was the only place he could stand after we had that child, the one that didn't make it.... We were going to call her Terra."

"Oh," I say to my shoes, incapable at this moment to understand irony.

"Your father and I always thought she was going to be a swimmer the way she kicked against my stomach," my mother says, stretching out her toes to touch the end of the bed. "Your father changed after that... we all did and we can never go back." She smiles at me and touches my face here and here and says, "It's funny how things worked out, isn't it? I wonder what Terra would have thought of us now. I wonder what she would think of what's happening with us, me, you, your father. I wonder what colour her hair would have been in her 30s. I wonder what her laugh would have sounded like. Or whether she would have been a sad one like you... but thank God, THANK GOD, she passed away because she would have only taken some of my love for you away and you are the only one in this family that I trust and understand."

I lie on the bed beside her, hold her hand, the one with the tiny plastic tube coming out of it, and I listen, realizing as she goes on that my mother is the factory where liquid is processed. Her tears, her spit, her piss, all moving through her, around me, into the walls, the ceiling, spilling out of the window and onto the parking lot, into the streets and everywhere while she speaks louder and louder about how much she loves me and she really does because I'm her only son, I'm the one she trusts and dreams and cries about and I will always, always tell her the truth no matter what and I stare at her watery eyes, her words turning over and over in my mind and it's all I can do to keep from screaming and screaming and screaming. What's the point? What is the fucking point? I AM SOLID GODDAMMIT!

But I pat her hand and stroke her hair and say nothing.

And I leave. Solid. But I'm not.

In three years my mother will be dead. Rejection.

In five years I lose my father. Stroke.

In-between, my wife. Miscarriage and divorce.

I'm older now and *my* kidneys are giving out. But my wine collection is growing.

No child. Oh I think about it all the time. What was, what could have been. Birthday cards and swimming lessons and "Look, Dad, look... no hands, no hands." A marching band. A piano lesson. A man selling ice-cream. A broken arm. A nose bleed. A long bedtime story finally coming to an end.

My wife, my ex-wife, occasionally sends me scotch because she thinks I could use a drink now and then. But I don't drink anymore. What's the point? She never re-married. Either.

I still have the photo. Terra. She would have been 37 today. She would have been a terrific mother... or a rotten one. She might have liked me. Or not. She might have been a poet. Or not.

What's left of my family, my sisters, moved to the coast. The opposite coast. We don't talk much. Long-distance... you know how it goes. Anyway, I'm busy too. You know, paddling. My kayak is red. It's made for two, but fits one perfectly fine. Every day I take it out rain or shine. I need to fight the water, feel the surge rip at my arms and shoulders as I try to beat my time. Whatever that is. And I will. I'm digging deep right now. Pushing as hard as I can, stroke after stroke after stroke... days falling behind me like days do. This happens, and that happens and I am still alone. Still alone. Yeah, you bet. But you go on, wave after wave trying to find some calm water. And then out in the middle of the bay, out in the middle of nowhere...

Water music up.

There. It's all around us. A river. A spring. A swell. The tide moving in. Rain, blessed, blessed rain, dripping down my face, down my neck and under my clothes soaking me through to the core, filling me, washing me, taking me apart piece by piece, molecule by molecule until there is nothing, nothing left and I am finally, finally dissolved. Christ...

He tries to compose himself.

There.... There.... Happy now? Shit.... Well... Okay. Fine... fine. Great.

I just want to.... I could.... No. No. This is it. This is really the end. That's all. I'm empty. Finished. Through. Done. Finally. Yeah.

Be as sad as you want.

The MAN picks up the glass of water and slowly drinks it. He puts the glass down, composes himself and waits as music builds and lights fade.

The end.

Between Mothers

Between Mothers was produced in February 2002 at Performance Works in Vancouver as part of Solo Collective's production *A Three Way*. It featured Megan Leitch as Rachael, directed by Tom McBeath, designed by Shaun August and staged managed by Lesley Humphrey. It was produced by Johnna Wright and Aaron Bushkowsky. This show was part of See Seven – an independent theatre initiative featuring the best of independent productions in Vancouver.

— • — **Setting** — • —

Rachael (37ish) sits on a bench in a park wearing a long coat.

BETWEEN MOTHERS

RACHAEL is anxious about the phone. Very anxious. She is nearly willing it to ring but perhaps we are not aware of this. We might hear wind.

RACHAEL
(to her cell phone) Okay. That's enough of that.

A moment.

Come on... let's go. Come on.

A moment.

Fuck you. I've never liked you anyway.

Another moment.

I guess it's obvious. I need professional help.

A woman in a brown turtleneck takes notes as I speak

you have a problem with transformation that's all

she says through her teeth. Alien mother. Nobody gets you anymore. Nobody wants you. Horrible, really. Oh well. I'm still young. Sort of.

My therapist... been through this before apparently with a daughter who left her for some bastard but let's not go there right now she says into her pen clicking now smiling and clicking reaching out like this and slightly pinching me oh exploration is dangerous isn't life full of surprises and let me tell you something about daughter number two no you're not ready to hear this are you ha ha ha

My therapist then tells me... it will soon be over.

This transformation of becoming something else.

This fucking journey I'm on.

She says forget about what's going on around me.

Forget about people and things and accidents and incidents.

Who said what and why. What happened when.

It's all up to me.

Who I am, right?

What I want, right?

Right. Eighty-five dollars an hour to hear that horse shit.

And where did it really get me?

She pours herself some scotch.

Well, it got me here... wherever here is. And it got me more of this scotch. This scotch from...

She reads the label.

...Russia that some people would call vodka,which my mother first got me to try when I was 12 which I in turn got Sandra, my daughter, to try when she was 12. Kids need a touch just to know.

So I was told... by my mother. Who really is out there. I put her away, finally. Just in a home with other confused mothers. Oh yeah, I know... how could I? How does it make me feel? I go there. I see them. The endless rows of wrinkled, used mothers lining the halls like rice paper and I feel... I feel like ironing them all out. It's all going to be okay, really... Mother. Trust me.

To the phone:

Anytime now!

Nothing. She takes off her coat.

The first therapist I tried... the one before the one I'm with now... I'm in her special therapy room and I hear this wind the whole time I'm there... wind coming through the cracks, wind at the window, wind under the door... I can't talk... I can't think.... "Fuck," I say, "What's with the wind today?"

"Oh, that's my tape. Most clients find it pleasing."

Well, I don't.

"Sounds like you're running from your problems," she says.

No, I'm running from your tape, okay?

"I sense your anger," she says.

Good, I say. Then I leave.

When I ran away from home, and I ran away a lot, there was nowhere to run to. A field of clover, a quarter-section of summer fallow, the barn, the next farm. Very boring. Like trying to escape Jello. So I had to come back. Back to the yellow house where my father was waiting for me... waiting to make it all up to me... whatever that meant. And usually it meant a lot. Like more pretty dresses, higher heels and redder lipstick. I was 14... but this was in a time when.... Well, you know. It was different back then. Our parents didn't have the benefits of therapy. Everybody was screwed up on the farm... although we were all very healthy.

My father always took me in his lap and told me that having a good sense of humour would get me out of almost any problem. Eventually, all my little jokes piled up around me like a big black wall, my husband turned red and start yelling, "You're killing me, you know that!"

Ha.

(to herself:) I'm right here. Right here.

My mother, who I hated because she had the misfortune of being my mother, always told me that if I was going to be too mad or too happy I should just go to my room. So I spent most of my teens in my bedroom reading *Sweet Sixteen* and *Psychology Today*. When I finally got out, I married my father. You know what I mean. A guy like my father. Because I thought I knew.... I was nineteen. Three years later I had his kid. Years and years together and then... bang. You know how it goes.

Then he gets to take Sandra every second weekend.

"Do you know how much I'm drinking?"

My kid, that's what's coming out of her mouth now. Can you believe this?

"Do you know how much I'm drinking? Look at me! Look at my face."

What did I know? What?

Far Mom. She called me Far Mom. Sandra did. Used to say it from the far side of the room like she had fluff in her mouth or something.

I couldn't talk. I didn't want to. I was drinking. A lot. So I was in my head, which is perfectly normal because it is *my* head, and she didn't understand. Far Mom, she said. I am sending you signals, Mother. Signals. Hey, don't just sit there and blink. I'm over here. Over here... over... here.

Blue dolphin eyes and blonde hair. Nervous fingers... strong hands... my face, broad and...

She's me. But not so tough. We don't have a lot in common. I watch TV, she reads books. I go to therapy, she does these astrology readings. She has a nasty streak... I fucking don't.

"Over here... over here."

Some people say I could be her sister. I don't look... my age. Which isn't very old. Is it?

"What are we doing, Mother? What's going on?"

All these questions she had. A man does this and a father does that.

"What's normal, Mom? What?"

Life and love. The usual teen-age stuff. Sure, you have to expect this.

"Do you love me? Do you?"

I started this mother thing too soon.... Who has kids at twenty-three today? Most of my friends... well, people I know, they're just starting and they're in their 40s. I guess they're having kids and retiring at the same time. It's more relaxing I'm sure.

"Do you really know how I feel? Ask."

Okay. Okay... I just want you to know, Sandra, I have these pills.... The doctor tells me I'm grinding my teeth at night, it wakes me up and I suddenly think there's somebody in the room with me. In the dark.

"You are fucking me up even more, Mother. And guess why. Guess."

They stopped working, I tell her. These stupid pills. Although I haven't tried them as a group... yet.

"I can leave at any time, Mother."

I laugh, friends tell me my eyes are turning red.

Well, not friends, acquaintances.

Well... neighbours, actually.

I tell them it's not me... it's not me... I mean, look at the cards I got dealt... look at the people that I love... they shouldn't be doing this... it's not right.... This is before I got hooked on "Oprah." I love that bald-headed therapist she has on her show. He's very understanding and forthright, is that a good word? And even a little sexy, I guess. He's so well rounded and kind and looks like he smells nice too. Although I can't imagine having sex with him.

My therapist... my person... tells me I'm on an exciting journey to become grounded. Electrifying even. I tell her to fuck off. She's a little shocked.

Most therapists become therapists because their marriages fell apart and they like giving advice to other people whose marriages are also falling apart. They've become experts and they're all very, very unhappy and they're perfectly satisfied with that because that's what they get paid for.

I told my therapist there's birth, then death and in between there's therapy.

She said, can we have a session without deflection, please? I said, I don't know, can we?

Ha.

She takes a drink.

I've stuck with this therapist because she reminds me of my mother. She also tells me to be... proactive. I haven't really been active in my life, I tell her and you want me to skip a step?

You can do it, sister, she says

Although to be clear... my mother would never use a word like proactive.

I don't remember the kind of words she used when I was a teenager but I remember her looks. You never forget those. No way.

Once from across the room my father told her she was stupid for buying flowers we grew in our garden anyway... I was right there, right there beside the sink drying the dishes.

"How... how could you be so incredibly stupid, woman? Knucklehead, idiot, fool..."

And she let all the air out of her like this...

She caught my eye and then turned away. Left me looking out at the window.

"What are you staring at, little miss?"

My dad's voice somewhere behind. And me, just standing there.

Little miss.

Little miss...

Funny... his exact words.

To the phone:

Come on... come on.

Help me.

The rest of the day my mother stayed in her garden, hiding behind the swaying sunflower heads. I pushed the stalks aside but she always moved away... why are you running from me? I didn't do anything. It wasn't me.

I complained to my dad and he swept me up into his bear arms and said, that's okay, never mind her, I got you now, don't I?

Joey got Sandra every second weekend. Six days a month. Every month. Year after year. Crying times. Those weekends. That's what Sandra told me. "Don't you get it? Don't you understand what's going on here?"

Oh come on. He's just trying to be nice to you, I said. A fancy dinner is nice. A new dress is nice. A make-over is nice. And he was very nice...

I would have done anything to get that man back into my life. Oh I know... how very dysfunctional of me. But as a mother... a reasonably young mother... you want to avoid putting "single" in front of all that. You want to avoid the chat lines or sitting alone pretending to read at Starbucks...

So I told Sandra. Go out with your father... try to have some fun.

What did I know? What do I know? Joey is funny. He has charm. Warm hands. And great laugh. And he made me feel good and on occasion, he made me feel very good.

Never marry a firefighter.

I should have listened to my mother. But then her mother told her never to marry a farmer and she did. And her mother's mother told her mother never to marry a butcher and she did. There's a pattern to it. It involves meat.

"I don't care what your mother said, you're *my* mother... say something different! And don't try to be funny."

What? What then? I'm dying over here, okay. I have no idea what you're...

And poof. She's gone. My girl.

She's young, I said. They disappear on you. It's not your fault. But it has to be somebody's. Right?

My therapist—the woman in the turtleneck—she tells me to pretend the chair is my ex-husband.

HA!

She kicks over the chair.

She says, Lucky I wasn't sitting in that.

I say, I thought you were.

She doesn't laugh. She squishes her face up into one of these...

She makes a face.

...then takes more notes.

We don't kick the chair again. We meaning me.

My therapist tells me she's my person. I say, my person, you're charging me way too much. She does the squish face again, says I'm just between mothers. My mother, dying of wrinkles and other things, in the home. My daughter, maybe pregnant, somewhere out there, out of my home, giving me wrinkles.

Why? Why did it happen this way? It seemed harmless enough. A normal day. I'm sitting at home watching "Who Wants to Be a Millionaire" when she says, Daddy always tries to look up my dress.

What dress, I say.

I'm serious, she says.

Now, the thing about this confession. Well, the first thing I thought was... Joey didn't mean it. He's just giving her an odd compliment. That's all. I mean, she's 15, 16 – she's an attractive girl. Woman. I... I look at her legs all the time. She says he says she has my legs. I say, Great, that's where they went.

Funny mother, she says. Funny.

A moment.

So I call Joey, I'm going to be proactive, right? My therapist will love this. I ask Joey, Excuse me, but what's going on with our daughter?

I can't imagine, he says. Let's meet for lunch. His treat, he says. One of those restaurants with ceiling fans and young female servers who don't wear bras, have tons of make-up and have their whole lives in front of them. They think their beauty will save them in the end... somehow. We all start off that way, don't we?

I order the garlic ribs. I don't care if I smell around Joey. In fact I prefer it. The young blonde server bounces up and runs for the kitchen and I'm left with my ex and he's staring at my chest.

I say "if my tits could talk, Joey, we'd still be married."

He smiles this... well, he has a nice smile and he says, "you've still got it and here's another thing... you're still beautiful."

"I am," I say.

"That's you alright," he says.

"But it's fading," I say.

"Right," he says. "I don't believe you."

A moment. We still have this moment. It happens. So I ruin it.

"Why are you looking up my daughter's dress?"

"What? Come on.... Shit." He hunkers down over his rolls.

I say, you didn't answer my question.

"Look, I just appreciate her beauty."

The thing is about my ex. Well, I know when he is lying because his ears turn red. Really red. And his ears are really, really big. He can get HBO on them.

A moment.

I'm getting less and less funny as I go on and I know it. Maybe it's all part of getting grounded. Like my therapist. My person. Nothing is funny to her anymore. I think my father was known for his sense of humour although I can't—for the life of me—remember a single funny thing he ever did. He picked up my dog by his ears once and laughed. But maybe that's not a good example... "ANSWER MY QUESTION, JOEY!"

My ex sits across from me with his big red ears and I'm waiting. "Come on... come on.... What did you do to her? My baby. My only child."

"What?" he shrugs. "What?"

"Don't you dare, don't you dare – goddammit! She's 16 years old and you've had her every second weekend since she's been 12. Our daughter. The one who painted butterflies on the fridge and... and slit her wrists. What did you do? What?! And I'm not going to ask you again."

Another moment. One of those you could pack a couple of hours of nothing into. He just sits there, not chewing anymore, just sits there and starts shrinking... literally shrinking and it's at that very moment, right there, right there, the server, who can't be any older than 19, arrives and his eyes catch her legs and then slowly, her chest, moving then up and down her skinny body and my God, my God, my ex-husband is oggling her and he catches me catch him and just smiles and shrugs and I take those garlic ribs and I throw them and the plate hits him on the forehead, CLANG, right between the eyes and I hear myself screaming.... "You bastard... you bastard.... You will never see her again. Or me. Do you understand? You fucking creep!"

And I leave. My dignity creeps behind me... in the shadow of my heart.

Shit.

When I get home, my child is gone. A note. Oh yes, she is still responsible.

"Dear Mom, I know you went out for dinner with Dad and I know you'll probably come home and tell me it's nothing. But I can't take it anymore... can't take his weekend visits or you doing nothing.... So I'm sorry, I got to go. I'm old enough to do this, please remember that, I will always love you, Mom, no matter what and I will always remember the birthday you said I might be special and made me cake and those other memories I can't remember anymore. Your daughter Sandy. P.S.: I think my boyfriend Jake—you know, the one with the cute tattoo of Satan—got me pregnant."

I made up the part about Satan, I think.

Anyway, that was a few days ago. I haven't heard from her since. You'd think she'd know better... you'd think she'd know that I'm going crazy. Shit.

I visit my mother in the home. I explain things. I go on and on and suddenly, for the first time in my life I hear myself asking her what to do.

"What? What, Mother, what should I do?"

"You know things, right. Very smart. Very independent. Used to ride your bike to market in a yellow dress and gum-boots. Wore Dad's old hard-hat for a helmet. A real rebel, that's you. Rode on the sidewalks all the time. Screw pedestrians, right? Once, remember this, you came in with these bloody elbows... I asked what happened and you said something about hitting a poodle... and scrambled eggs. I'm positive it was funny. Positive."

"Funny girl. Particular," my Dad always said. Remember?

"Mother? Mother? Come on. You've got to help me. You've got to."

"What? What? Come on... come on, Mother. What should I do? What? A daughter does this and a woman does what?" But she blinks and she blinks and she licks her lips and... that's it... that's all.

Pop, pop, pop.... A series of small strokes. Vacuuming in the middle of the night, going over and over the same old stain in the carpet and there I am by the door trying to yell over the racket.

"Mother? Mother?! I'm over here! Over here!"

   A moment.

I sign the papers. The ones that say, if they go, don't bother. Let her go... let her go. Fine, I will. They said they would call if... well, either way, they would call. They always do.

And Sandra... she should.

Between mothers. That's me. I guess.

   A moment.

I go home and lie on the couch, munch ice-cubes and watch reruns of "Law and Order" but I don't know what's going on. I mean, the new lawyer is way too beautiful and everybody's so fucking intense and I'm trying to concentrate but the guy upstairs wears cowboy boots and he's a heel walker, right, and I haven't paid the cable bill or the phone bill by the way and I'm lying there... just lying there... developing a rash and God I wished I smoked again and what's with this show... every fucking scene is like one minute long and it's all zooming past me... everything is going blink, blink, blink and outside there's this yelling and yelling and yelling... what is it with people in co-ops...?

Get a life, you morons! And take that knife away from your kid!

Emergency session. A hundred bucks an hour. I don't care. "Get me in now. NOW GOD-DAMMIT!"

Putting on her coat.

I have trouble sounding normal. My voice is thinning out... I feel fat. Fatter. I've noticed more lines on my face. When I smile, my ears hurt and I don't know if you noticed but my hair just sits there.

My person nods and nods.

Sandra is gone. My mother is gone. My phone will not ring. And I don't want it to ring. But I do. What is happening to me? What is happening? My God... please tell me! I am dying inside. I am drying up and crumbling apart and you've got to help me. You've just got to! And now my right ear is about to explode because she is filling the room with a black hole of a pause you know the kind you just have to fill somehow and i am beside myself thinking what do i want what do i want because i have a problem apparently with transformation and my kid who is somewhere out there in the great unknown my daughter my lovely daughter who I guess also has a problem with transformation but apparently this is perfectly normal for mothers because this is exactly what we women signed up for and we shouldn't be surprised that humans are fully capable of becoming anything they want to and to love somebody to really love somebody is to breathe stuff that can apparently kill us me you with the slightest shift of a breeze and that is what i want of course absolutely without a doubt this is what i want to love to live to die to at least try oh God oh God i really want to try you have to believe me help me help me please help me i am changing and the world is changing and everything isn't fucking normal and i can't take it anymore please, please help me and i am saying this as loud as I can and she barely moves barely blinks

clicks her tongue

aahhh she says

aaahhhh

welcome home

welcome home

Fuck... fuck... fuck...

The next thing I know I've got a banana and a latte and I'm standing in the sky train station.... One train goes by... another train goes by... another.... They go by pretty fast. It's about fifteen feet to the edge of the platform. Ten feet... five feet... two foot...

A young mother pushing a baby carriage... big wheels... the kind joggers use... she's moving it back and forth... rocking the baby, I guess.... Over there... she sees me from over there... the other side... tracks between us.... Trains go by. A blur.

She's still there. Rocking. Her baby... I guess it's crying... but she's not looking down at it.... The wind... another train... my hair... like it's full of snakes... anticipates.... I take another step... and this mother... this young woman... she holds up her finger.... Shhhhhhhhhh.

(to herself) Shhhhh. Shhhhh.

> *A moment. The phone rings, but she first doesn't know where it is. Finally, she snaps out of it and scrambles to dig it out of her coat. But by the time she gets it in her hand it stops ringing. A moment. She gathers herself.*

Okay.... Okay...

Shit.

> *She begins to rock slightly.*

Right. Okay.

> *A moment where all hope seems to have faded. She is deflated, defeated, empty. Then her phone rings again. Hope returns. She pulls it toward her chest, it rings again, then she pulls it to her ear and answers it.*

"Yes."

Aaron Bushkowsky, a graduate of the Canadian Film Centre, has been produced and published in several genres: film, poetry, theatre, prose, and non-fiction. His book of poetry *ed and mabel go to the moon* was nominated for the Dorothy Livesay Award for Best Book of Poetry in BC. His latest book of poems, *Mars is for Poems*, garnered critical acclaim ("Aaron Bushkowsky travels further in his imagination than any other Canadian poet." *Vancouver Sun*). His short stories have been published across Canada. His short film, "The Alley," which aired on CBC, won the National Screen Institute drama prize, and was nominated for six Leos (BC Film Awards).

Aaron's many plays, which include the award-winning *Strangers Among Us*, have been produced throughout Canada. He has also been nominated for Jessie Richardson Theatre Awards for Outstanding Original Play for five years in a row, winning two. His latest play *One Last Kiss*, directed by Roy Surette received its world premiere at Victoria's Belfry Theatre in January 2004 and was also produced by the Vancouver Playhouse shortly afterward. Aaron's *The Dead Reckoning*, also produced by The Vancouver Playhouse, was nominated for a Jessie Richardson Theatre Award for writing. *Soulless*, will be produced by Rumble Theatre in April 2004, another world premiere. Aaron has served as playwright-in-residence at Touchstone Theatre, The Playhouse, Rumble Theatre and as a resident film-writer at the Canadian Film Centre in Toronto. He has a new book of prose upcoming, *The Vanishing Man* (Cormorant Books, 2004).

Aaron completed his MFA in Creative Writing at UBC and teaches playwriting and filmwriting at Langara College's Studio 58, Douglas College, Playwrights Theatre Centre, and the Vancouver Film School. He is the co-artistic director of Solo Collective, an emerging Vancouver theatre company noted for producing new Canadian plays, particularly monologues. The company has been nominated for many Jessie Richardson Theatre awards, including two for Outstanding Production. Aaron lives in Vancouver with his Aussie Shepherd Frankie and his feral cat, Mabel.

"It's me."

"I know... I know."

"I know. No, it's me. No, I know it's me..."

Lights slowly fade.

The end.